# Last Laughs

## Prehistoric Epitaphs

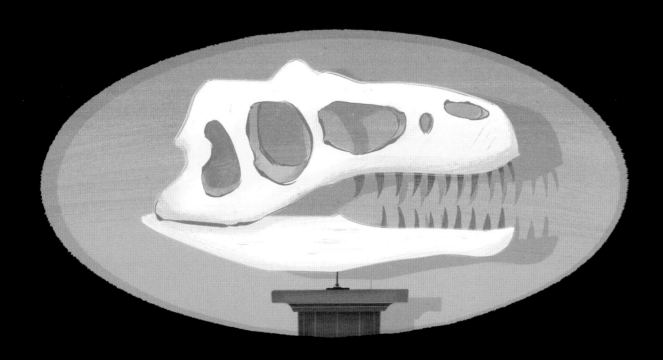

J. Patrick Lewis and Jane Yolen
*Illustrated by* Jeffrey Stewart Timmins

Charlesbridge

# Contents

4

Prof. M. Piltdown
Paleontologist

# Last Laugh Layers

Here the ancient seas are dry.
Here the grave sites all pile high.
Here Jurassic, Cenozoic;
all dead fossils, some heroic.
Some in pieces, tooth and nail,
lie buried in the local shale.

The dino wake starts. Goodness gracious,
time to party through Cretaceous.
Here's a glass, so meteoric,
raised to toast the prehistoric.
Do we miss them? Now and then.
But we survivors say, "Amen."

5

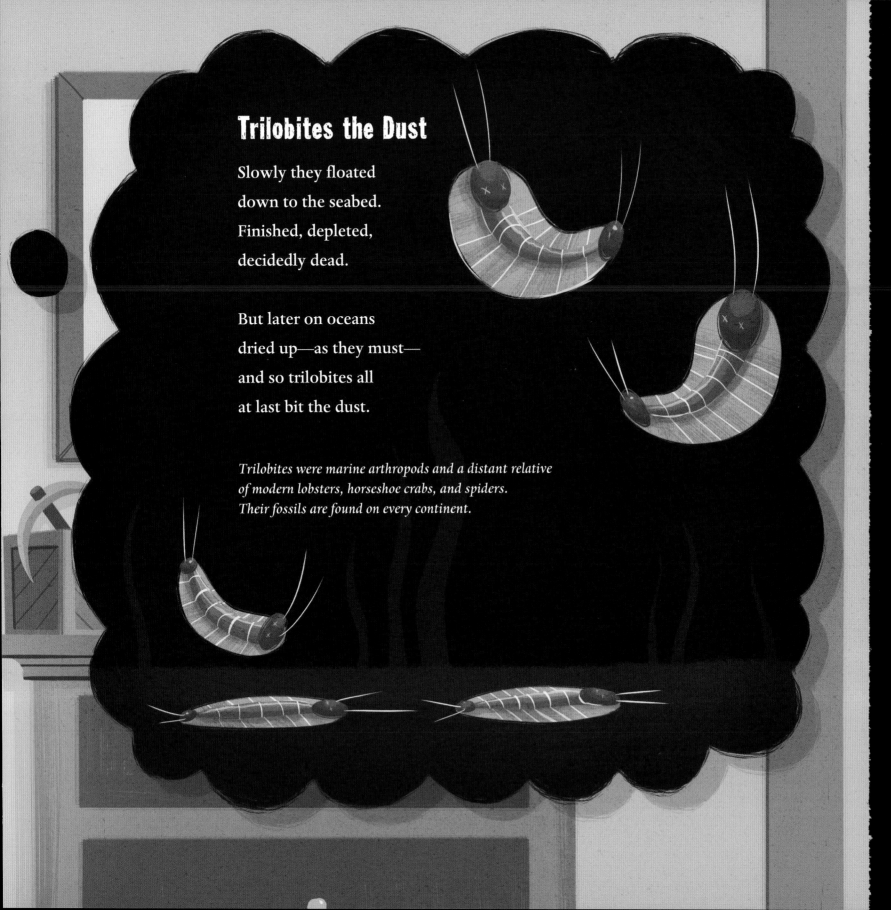

# Trilobites the Dust

Slowly they floated
down to the seabed.
Finished, depleted,
decidedly dead.

But later on oceans
dried up—as they must—
and so trilobites all
at last bit the dust.

*Trilobites were marine arthropods and a distant relative
of modern lobsters, horseshoe crabs, and spiders.
Their fossils are found on every continent.*

# Plesiosaur Sticks His Neck Out

Swimming on the ocean floor,
long-necked, green-decked plesiosaur
stuck his neck out once too often—
a Pictish blow no one could soften.
There should have been a mighty mess,
except it happened in Loch Ness.

*The plesiosaur lived in the ocean, not a lake, and it looked as we
imagine the Loch Ness monster. It became extinct sixty-five million
years ago (long before the Picts inhabited Scotland).*

8

# Pterrible Pterosaur Pterminated

Like a snake

and a bat,

I'm a bit of a brat.

I'm a tooth

and a bone

underneath a headstone.

Now all you can see

is this painting of me!

*Although they are often called dinosaurs, pterosaurs actually belong to a group of prehistoric reptiles called Pterosauria. They could reach very high speeds (perhaps seventy-five miles per hour) and travel thousands of miles.*

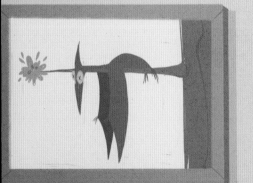

Prof. M. Piltdown
Paleontologist

# *Diplodocus* Has a Lump in Her Throat

Let the pain in my neck
be a lesson to you—
never swallow a shrub
that you cannot chew.

Diplodocus *was one of the longest dinosaurs on record. Its*
*enormous neck allowed it to forage deep into forests.*

## *Allosaurus*, Rest in Pieces

Who knows in which century my bag o' bones

was buried by this monument of stones?

Where am I on the ancient critter list?

Go ask your friendly paleontologist.


*Allosaurus ("strange lizard") was a large and common*
*predator. It was 28–40 feet long and weighed three tons.*

## *Iguanodon,* Alas Long Gone

Iguano dawned,

Iguano dined,

Iguano done,

Iguano gone.

*First discovered in England in 1822, the giant Iguanodon usually walked on four legs, but it could run on two legs to escape predators or gather food.*

## *Minmi* Moans in the Outback

A small vegan dinosaur, *Minmi,*

once asked, "Why did ten raptors skin me?"

The armored tank said,

"See, I wasn't quite dead

till those dinosaurs stuck their beaks in me!"

*This armored, slow-moving vegetarian was found only in Australia and had bony protrusions along its head, back, stomach, legs, and tail.*

## SuperCroc Plot

Mother always told me, "Sarc,

leave your puncturation mark."

Her advice to me? "On hunts,

chew your fishy dinner . . . once."

But this lush life that we enjoyed

was ruined by an asteroid

that left all SuperCrocs like me

sunk in anonymity.

Sarcosuchus, *also known as SuperCroc, was as long as a city bus and ten times as heavy as the biggest crocodile today. SuperCrocs kept growing even as they got older.*

# Why No *Spinosaurus?*

With that huge sail stuck on my back,

you'd think that I was out of whack.

Still, I was monster of the 'hood—

which every creature understood.

Then rivers started going dry!

And when no dinner caught my eye,

what was a spinosaur to do

but shrivel up to a worm's-eye view?

Spinosaurus *was the largest known meat-eating dinosaur. The first-discovered set of* Spinosaurus *fossils was destroyed in a World War II bombing raid.*

## Too Much Velocity, *Velociraptor*

On the run, he thought too much,
this Einstein of the 'saurs.
He calculated chances
of escaping predators.

He stepped into a pothole.
He broke a leg or two,
which multiplied his chances
of becoming dino chew.

*This small, vicious, feathered raptor was no more than*
*three feet tall and weighed about thirty pounds.*
*Scientists think it was very smart or at least wily.*

## *Troodon*, a Snaggletoothed Youth

Born on Sunday,
Monday teething.
Tuesday morning,
heavy breathing.
Wednesday wasting
birds and lizards,
Thursday feasting,
fat on gizzards.
Friday ate a
rancid beast.
Saturday?
I was deceased.

Troodon *had a very big brain and was probably about
as smart as a modern ostrich. Scientists think this birdlike,
meat-eating creature stood three feet tall.*

18

# Tricera Blew Her Top

A vegetarian from the start,
she gobbled only greens.
She wasn't good at running
or at making awkward scenes.
Her horns were bone and keratin,
her teeth not meant to bite.
So when she met a hungry Rex
she ofttimes lost the fight.

*Triceratops had three horns made of bone covered in keratin (the protein in hair and fingernails). This plant-eating dinosaur was notable for its big head, which was one-third the length of its body.*

## Fossil Fuel: *Kol*

No oil is left in town—
each well, an empty hole.
But if you dig ten feet down . . .
Eureka! *Kol.*

Who wrote its final chapter?
Who put it in the ground?
Thanks to *Velociraptor,*
it's very rarely found.

*The only known fossil of the rare* Kol—*pronounced* coal—
*is a single, well-preserved foot. Because* Velociraptor *bones were
found in the same location, scientists have speculated that Kol's
main predator was the* Velociraptor.

# Fooling with *T. rex*

Some old 'saurus threw a bone,

told *T. rex* to bring it home.

Roared out, "Rexie, go and fetch it!"

*T. rex* raced around to catch it.

Lost his footing on a cliff,

guessed he soon would be a stiff.

Fell a yard and then a mile.

Wasn't found for quite a while.

*Though larger dinosaur bones have now been found,*
*Tyrannosaurus rex is still called "king of dinos."*
*An apex (top-level) predator, T. rex was forty feet long,*
*stood about twenty feet tall, and weighed seven tons.*

# Terror Bird Kicks the Bucket

Seven feet high,

he could not fly.

Though he tried—

it's how he died.

Still kicking as he fell off a mountain.

*There are a few different types of terror birds, some of which migrated from South America into North America. Scientists have long thought that they were carnivorous, but they may have been herbivorous.*

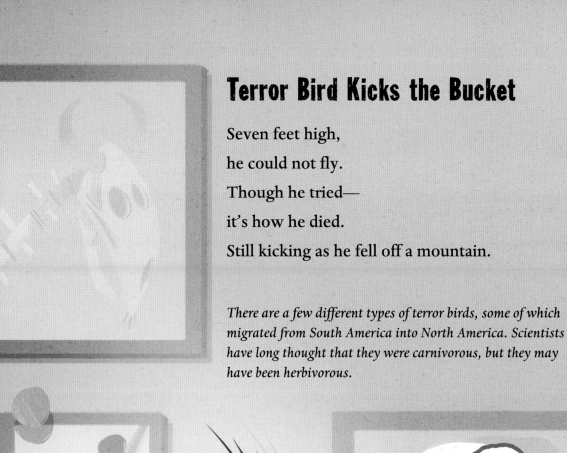

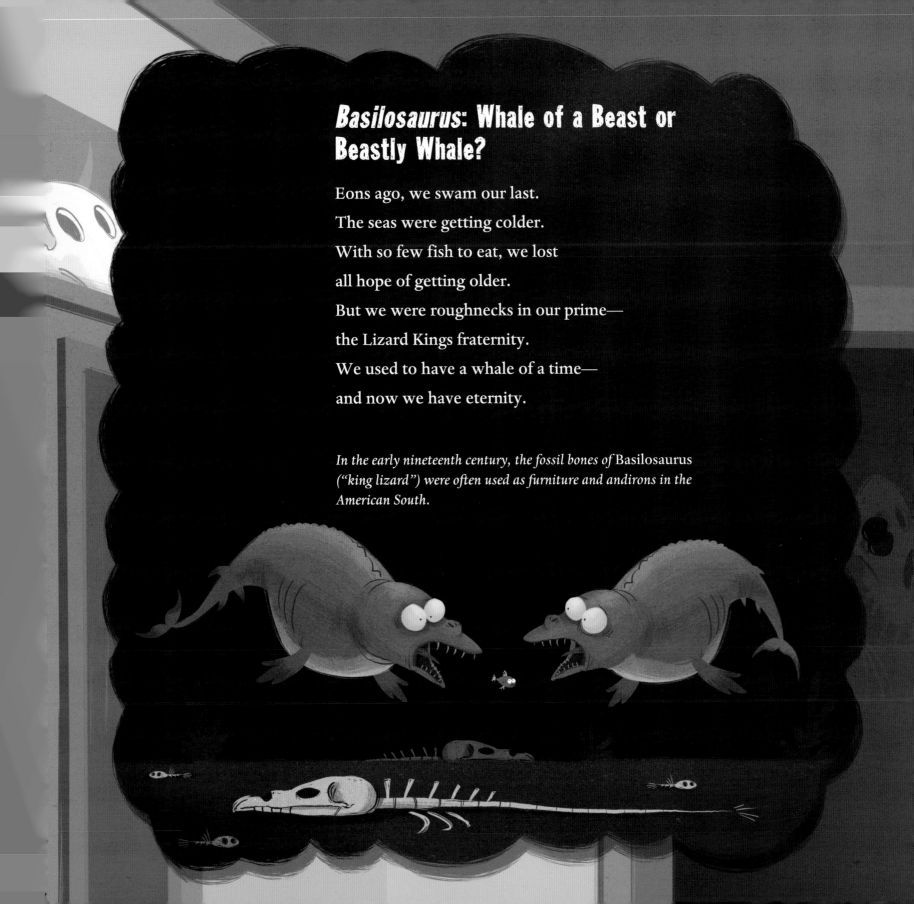

## *Basilosaurus*: Whale of a Beast or Beastly Whale?

Eons ago, we swam our last.

The seas were getting colder.

With so few fish to eat, we lost

all hope of getting older.

But we were roughnecks in our prime—

the Lizard Kings fraternity.

We used to have a whale of a time—

and now we have eternity.

*In the early nineteenth century, the fossil bones of Basilosaurus ("king lizard") were often used as furniture and andirons in the American South.*

## Scat, Old Saber-Toothed Cat

Tiger, tiger, hunting bright

near the tar pits, late at night.

Neither claws nor saber teeth

saved you from what lay beneath.

Stuck like that, you starved to death,

growling with your final breath.

*This large, meat-eating predator is related to modern cats. It was about one foot shorter than modern lions but two times as heavy.*

## Crying (Dire) Wolf

Chasing prey

into the mire.

Mud sucked feet.

A death most dire.

*With a scientific name (Canis dirus) meaning "fearsome dog," this carnivorous animal was the size of a gray wolf. However, its bite was more than twice as strong as the bite of the modern animal.*

# Holy Moly, Woolly Mammoth

Woolly mammoth in a muddle,

feet sunk deep in tarry puddle.

Needed pulley, not invented.

Woolly now wholly lamented.

*A relative of the modern elephant, the woolly mammoth had enormous, curved tusks and lived on plants. Its only natural predator was the saber-toothed cat. Later on, humans wiped out the woolly mammoth through hunting.*

# Dinosaur Doomstones

If you should stumble on fossils like us,
some small, some impossibly big—
go ahead, you're entitled to make a great fuss!
Now take out your shovel. You dig?

Scraping the dirt from a miniature mound
could lead to something much bigger,
and if it's a dinosaur burial ground,
then bravo, you eager grave digger.

Once you have found an unusual bone,
Draw an outline of it on a graph.
Pick out a sign, a forever doomstone—
Now write a dino epitaph!

29

## A Little About Layers

The bones of dead prehistoric animals—fish, mammals, birds, reptiles, and more—were buried by ancient seas, volcanic ash and lava, and primordial ooze. The oldest fossils and bones are found in the bottom layers, with newer fossils piled on top of them. Some species existed in more than one era, while others managed to survive for just part of one era. We have written poems about only a few ancient creatures—there are hundreds more throughout the fossil record. Writing poems about all of them would take more than a single poet's lifetime. Maybe *you* could write your own epitaphs to round out our collection!

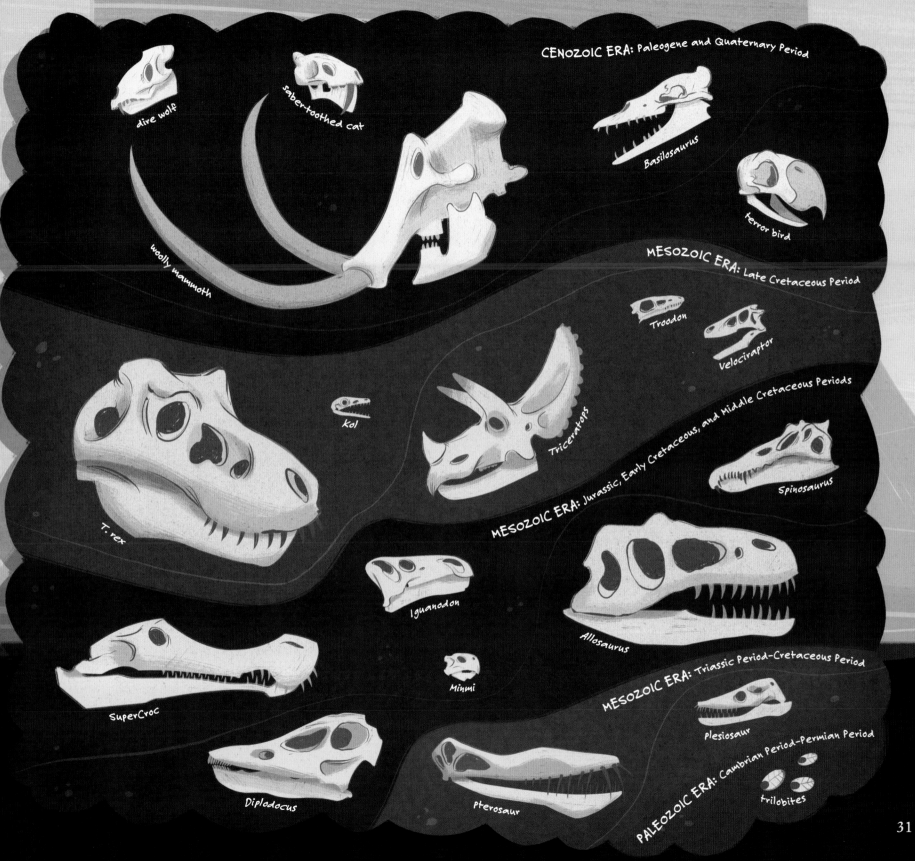

CENOZOIC ERA: Paleogene and Quaternary Period

dire wolf

saber-toothed cat

Basilosaurus

terror bird

woolly mammoth

MESOZOIC ERA: Late Cretaceous Period

Troodon

Velociraptor

Kol

Triceratops

Spinosaurus

T. rex

MESOZOIC ERA: Jurassic, Early Cretaceous, and Middle Cretaceous Periods

Iguanodon

Allosaurus

SuperCroc

Minmi

MESOZOIC ERA: Triassic Period-Cretaceous Period

Diplodocus

pterosaur

Plesiosaur

trilobites

PALEOZOIC ERA: Cambrian Period-Permian Period

31

To Heidi Stemple, who came up with the prehistoric idea, and to Yolanda, who saw it in its Eocene mode and made it into a historic book—J. Y.

To Sanay, Selis, Tola, and the recently discovered Hooded Claw—J. P. L.

For Myrtlesaurus Rex—J. S. T.

Published by Charlesbridge
85 Main Street
Watertown, MA 02472
(617) 926-0329
www.charlesbridge.com

**Library of Congress Cataloging-in-Publication Data**
Names: Yolen, Jane, author. | Lewis, J. Patrick, author. | Timmins, Jeffrey Stewart, illustrator.
Title: Last laughs : prehistoric epitaphs / Jane Yolen and J. Patrick Lewis; illustrated by
  Jeffrey Stewart Timmins.
Description: Watertown, MA : Charlesbridge, [2017]
Identifiers: LCCN 2016009218 (print) | LCCN 2016015772 (ebook) | ISBN 9781580897068 (hard cover) |
  ISBN 9781607349211 (ebook) | ISBN 9781607349228 (ebook pdf)
Subjects: LCSH: Dinosaurs—Juvenile humor. | Dinosaurs—Juvenile poetry.
Classification: LCC PN6231.D65 Y65 2017 (print) | LCC PN6231.D65 (ebook) | DDC 818/.602—dc23
LC record available at https://lccn.loc.gov/2016009218

Printed in China
(hc) 10 9 8 7 6 5 4 3 2 1

Illustrations done using Adobe Photoshop
Display type set in Tuzonie by HBI at Aah Yes Fonts
Text type set in Dante MT by Adobe Systems Incorporated
Color separations by Colourscan Print Co Pte Ltd, Singapore
Printed by 1010 Printing International Limited in
  Huizhou, Guangdong, China
Production supervision by Brian G. Walker
Designed by Martha MacLeod Sikkema